The Sound of VICTORY

A Young Boy's Journey Through Hearing Loss and Sports

Alexander J. Narcisse

ISBN #: 979-8-218-35495-4

Cover and Interior Design: Creative Publishing Book Design

Dedicated to all children born with hearing loss and the Texas Hearing Institute.

This book is for young children, especially those with hearing loss. First, it is to show that children with hearing loss who wear hearing devices such as cochlear implants or hearing aids can play sports. Retention devices are key! I used sweatbands for tennis, basketball, and soccer. I used skull caps for football, baseball, rugby, and lacrosse. Second, you will notice the use of many onomatopoeia words throughout the book. This is to help the reader "hear" the action and make connections between the action and the sound.

Illustrator: Pictures originally photographed by Victor J. Narcisse III

Always reach for the sky because there is no limit. Follow the story about a young boy named Alex with an unbeatable spirit who was born with hearing loss. Alex wears cochlear implants to help him hear. Alex plays as many sports as he wants because there is no stopping him-not even being deaf.

Alex likes to play tennis. Can you hear him WHACK the tennis ball?

Baseball is one of Alex's favorite pastimes. Do you hear the POW when the bat hits the baseball?

Alex loves to swim when it is hot outside. Can you hear him SPLASH in the water?

Alex loves making baskets. Can you hear the ball SWISH when it hits the net?

Watching Alex play soccer is fun. He can really **KICK** the ball!

Alex had so much fun when he hit the slopes to ski. Can you hear him WHOOSH down the mountain?

Alex likes to SOAR the football through the air while doing the quarterback shuffle. Can you hear the grass CRUNCH?

Alex is practicing his martial arts kicks. Can you hear him getting ready to **CRACK** the board?

BEEP BEEP! Move out the way. Alex is on the run in Rugby.

POW! Kaboom! Jab! Wheels! Lacrosse is Alex's favorite sport. Can you hear the CLANG when the ball hits the crossbar?

Over the years, Alex has navigated playing sports while wearing cochlear implants, but it has not been easy. Through this journey, Alex has learned the importance of embracing his differences and the power of resilience. Alex's message to all children who have hearing loss is: "You can do it. Don't let your hearing loss prevent you from playing sports."

ABOUT THE AUTHOR

Alexander "Alex" Narcisse lives in Houston, Texas. Alex was born with mild to moderate hearing loss, which progressively diminished his hearing over time. He wore hearing aids beginning at 15 months and received his first cochlear implant at two years old. He was bimodal for several years before he received his second cochlear implant at seven years old. Alex attended the Melinda Webb School as a toddler where he learned to listen and speak. Alex has been mainstreamed, with accommodations, since four years old. Currently, he is a sophomore at a college preparatory private high school. He is an honor roll student who played Freshman football and is on the Junior Varsity Lacrosse team. His favorite subjects are math and history. He is a dedicated student of WW 2 history, especially the battles in the Pacific Theatre. In his free time, Alex enjoys hanging out with friends, playing video games, building Legos and spending time with his younger brother, Ethan, and their beagle, John John.